Voices and Passions

by

Abdulai Walon-Jalloh

SLWS

Voices and Passions

Copyright © 2015 by Abdulai Walon-Jalloh
All rights reserved.

ISBN: 978-99910-54-38-4

Sierra Leonean Writers Series

DEDICATION

This work is dedicated to my country
Sierra Leone and its people.

INTRODUCTION

In the past, Sierra Leonean literary writers had struggled for survival especially in the light of other countries whose literature had been very prolific and widely read by a good number of their indigenes and foreigners. Among the protracted challenges associated with that struggle were only few Sierra Leoneans were interested in writing and there was the lack of the necessary impetus. Even when those literary pieces were published, there was no ready market for them to be sold as Sierra Leoneans then preferred reading literature from other countries.

However, at the dawn of the 21st Century, the paradigm shifted and that saw the rise of younger Sierra Leonean writers who were very much desperate to make Sierra Leonean Literature not only widespread in the country but also transcend borders. This new wave brought about a proliferation of the three literary genres by Sierra Leonean writers.

The University of Sierra Leone was not complacent about the new wave and lecturers, who are talented in writing, joined the blaze as they too wanted to share their remarkable experiences with those near and far.

The present collection is the maiden edition of a thorough and focused work of one of the lecturers in the Language Studies Department at Fourah Bay College – University of Sierra Leone.

Simply written, the poet brings out a good number of experiences (both personal and general) which are highly descriptive, thus making them very compelling to readers. These past, present and future issues described are neatly woven in the different lines and stanzas of the collection which ultimately makes it one of high quality in Sierra Leonean poetry.

With a variety of rhythm and number of lines per stanza, the poet equally makes use of the different literary devices in order to make the reader thrilled from start to finish.

This collection is very much inspirational and as the reader flicks through its rich content, s/he may likely situate him/herself in one or many of the incidents mentioned or even recall remarkable events and places which include 4.27.61 and Kissy Brook.

Prince H. Kenny
Head of Department, Language Studies
Fourah Bay College
University Sierra Leone
July 2015

ENDORSEMENTS

Abdulai Walon-Jalloh's **Voices and Passions** brings us face to face with a poet who is concerned not only with what touches him personally, but also with issues that transcend race, frontier or sex: love, religion, happiness, corruption, politics and nature. We go on a journey with Walon-Jalloh In his debut collection of poetry, as his mind traverses over the places that have moulded his character and left an indelible imprint on his mind; The Sierra Leone Library Board, Kissy Brook, Fourah Bay College and Freetown. The most striking note of his verse is one of restraint, endowed on his poems not only by the matter-of-fact tone in which they are couched, but also in his delight in rhyme. The language of his poems is economical and the haunting beauty or tenderness of a handful of his poems is balm to our souls. His enduring love for Sierra Leone seeps through the pores of his verse and we leave his poems firmly convinced that this volume of poetry is a precursor to other volumes. Like John the Baptist, this volume is sent to prepare the way.

Elizabeth Lucy Kamara
Lecturer of English and Literature
Head of English Language Unit
Fourah Bay College, University of Sierra Leone.

Voices and Passions

In this haunting collection, Walon-Jalloh's pen comes alive. His themes ranging from the materialism and immorality which are the generic banes of modern societies, to yuletide, the beautiful sterility of Freetown, the birth pangs of nationhood, the differed dream of the Athens of West Africa, the ghastly cadavers that speak of man's propensity to do violence to his brother, the joys of motherhood, the loss of identity and the innocence of childhood encapsulate his inner psychological trauma informed by a desire to find an outlet for long bottled up anger. In the midst of this stanzaic trauma, he pursues his subject matter with an ease and craftsmanship that only a deft artist can. Kafkaesque but mundane, his adroitness with words holds the reader's breath as he explores with poignant frankness his firsthand experience of life in his native Freetown, the poignant beauty of his motherland and the joys of sorrows of his ill-fated compatriots. In this work his themes are as blistering and as variegated as the rawness with which he scythes his experiences. A word economist, Walon-Jalloh's work is an exercise in thematic variance that is the perfect initiation for those who crave after the terrible beauty written with the cadence of verse. **Voices and Passions** is a powerful debut that heralds the dawn of a career that will sparkle for many years to come.

Sheik Bakarr Kamara
Lecturer of Poetry and English
English Language Unit,
Department of Language Studies,
Fourah Bay College, University of Sierra Leone.

Contents

Dedication   i
Introduction   ii
Endorsements   iv

Poems

The Sierra Leone Library Board	1
Man against man	3
Nothing new	5
Not yet Christmas	7
Did I hear you say…?	8
Freetown	9
4. 27. 61	11
Fourah Bay College Mount Aureol	12
Kissy Brook	13
Pain no more	15
Under the Tree	17
The Mango Tree	19
The unreachable gleam	21
Wurrie	22
Differing sameness	23
Apart	24
The Rainy Season	25
Voices	27
Wing'd Chariot	28
Nightfall	29
Love	30
The Light	31
Reckoning	32
Free	33

Why the fuss?	34
Apart but not forever	35
Neneh (Mother)	36
What is my name?	37
Feet on wheels	38
Childhood	39
It's in your Eyes	40
The East-end	42
Market Borbor	44
Congo Dust	46
Sierra Leone at 48	48
Freetown Night	50
The wild	51
Moments of Glory	52
The distance	53
The Story of Life	54
Living Reality	56
The Road	58
Last Line of Defence	60
Dance in the forests	63
The Race	64
The Real Us	65
The Era of Men	66
The Baboon's Bottom	68
Sons of yester years	69
Happiness	70
Youths	71
Success	72
Where have they gone to?	73
The Fading	74

Abdulai Walon-Jalloh

Sierra Leone Library Board

What a squattish brilliance?
Of a sturdy character
Deposited at an intersection
Leading to numerous destinations

Your neighbours the foremost Gentlemen
Your gaze challenged by zealous pupils
As submissive ambitious knowledge-seekers wade
through
To endure the tormenting quiet of steadied thoughts

Though noisy motorists are about
Yet the cacophony is kept at bay
As zephyr oozes through your inlets
Filtering through the Masonic edifice

Oh! Semi-centenarian!
Your longevity amazes
The multitude far and wide
As you slide through better or worse

Your continued presence
Is generosity to all
Shared by all
Be it big or small

As the beneficiary army galore
So the employees never tire
Against shine or wet, heat or cold
As it becomes "keep it up"

Though your limited presence
Is agony for many
Thus your presence in their midst needn't delay
As the 'Land that we love' depends on it

Oh! Great semi-centenarian!
Continue the wondrous accent
As you take along your children in your stride
For there are more heights to be scaled.

Man against Man

It's in those
Who fight them
To release that
Stored in venom

They are nothing
As is something
To the thing
That is anything

Try as they may
Why are they about?
Dry are the winds
Permeating among them

With utter dismay
They surely display
In a wide array
Their characteristic folly

It's maximum self-annihilation
That issues from profound self-preservation
That's in the need of rampant mutilation
In a world capable of needless remorse

Unending torture
Is the future
For a current feature
In a canvass of pictures

Abdulai Walon-Jalloh

Man shall never learn
As man against man
Reverberates through the spine
With every quaking step
As the brilliant sun shows the way

Nothing New

Of palatial mansions, beautiful women and fancy cars
With too many rooms, undying lust and never-ending models
So much confusion, insatiate desires and one at expense of many
Costly repairs, unhealthy competition and heightened neglect

Nothing new
To what they knew
Yet hopes will renew
In the minds of the few

The fortresses in resolute minds
Shall not long be resolved
As edifices crumble, beauty fades and fancy dulls
Witness the derelictions, the desert roses and rumbling monstrosities

Nothing new
To what they knew
Yet hopes will renew
In the minds of the few

As the birds on the mango tree
Shall continue to observe as higher mortals self destruct
In the thick of darkness and under the transcendental beautiful sun
So their numbers and kind shall continue to wonder

Abdulai Walon-Jalloh

Nothing new
To what they knew
Yet hopes will renew
In the minds of the few

Not yet Christmas

Ah! It's not yet Christmas
Though the sheep are bleating
And church bells are ringing
It's not yet Christmas

Yet in our minds
And in our hearts
It could just be
So why despair?

Truth is, it's not yet…
Why is it so?
And with all this frenzy
It is yet Christmas

We can make thus
In character and activity
The mad rush could begin
And the family will settle in

Fact is, it is not yet…
In spite of the tranquil
And depleting birches
And the popping gifts…

I say, it's not yet Christmas

Did I hear you say…?

Yes indeed we are for them
Who are of our stem
Through the burdened spells
Ringing like church bells

We the faceless
Amidst the voiceless
With untiring bones
And perfect tones

Grace attends
Gripes galore
Diminishing happiness
Death dwells

Yet did I hear you say…?
Though with tireless toil
The tide we stay
As folks recoil
We are the ceaseless wonder
In hills and valleys over yonder
As pelting rains wander
Against the storms we don't surrender

Generations issue forth
Others surrender at our fort
With warmth we inspire
With caring we aspire

Yet did I hear you say…?

Freetown

Amidst turbulence
Raging schisms
Cataclysmic encounters
Rioting hues

A wavy shoreline
A snaky glare
An enlarged rear
An embossed terrain

Of exaggerated outbursts
A scintillating phalanx
Increasing literati
A riveting tale

A tale of gnashed teeth
Of bruised elbows
Guaranteed broken shins
And tainted hopes

Gore!
Tears!
Sweat!
Mirth!

Oh! Transcendental beauty!
Cast in thunderous climes
Of assured resilience
And a punctuating zephyr

Abdulai Walon-Jalloh

You are free
To the shackled hopeless
Searching for freedom
Land of the free

4. 27. 61

Amidst the wild merriments
In distant lands and climes
With deafening laughter and agreements
The newborn bursts forth in prime

With reluctance and regret
The request fulfilled
The sun shines forth
As inspired folks re-lived

Yet promises galore
The dreams fade
As nature ventures to explore
For aspiration within no longer abides

It's forlorn and awry
For no listeners attend
As lamentations multiply in cry
Your soothing presence you lend

Abdulai Walon-Jalloh

Fourah Bay College Mount Aureol

Approaching from the seafront
A lion is crouching at the front
An overbearing belch disguised in grunts
With large parched land and trees burnt

Wild hairs blown about
Extended ears standing to flout
Tensed claws ready for the bout
As grizzly rings on the neck begin to sprout

On the head an elongation
As wild characteristic boom in explosion
Of slow treacle of ants in upward progression
As in guaranteed slumber your projection

Busy ants about in every corner
As assured measure for the loner
Not often visits to the coroner
Busy ants rewarded by the commoner

Ubiquitous anthills dot the top
As they welcome every stop
Little is mentioned of the flop
As the littler ants on your back with a mop

Your eyes represent solace
For the few that can race
From a wild and warm embrace
Yours is a path of grief and grace

Kissy Brook

How snaky you are!
How unfathomable you are!
How soothing you are!
How pleasant you are!

In your embrace
Many receive grace
In your bosom
Many will blossom

With your presence
An increased sense
In elevated beauty
With little pity

With feet pattering
And hands splashing
Patters are pounding
And basins are dipping

Patient hands
Folded hands
For guys
On land

Your traffic shall never cease
For your essence will always please
As your never-ending breeze
Always accompanies the trees

Running through mountains
Traversing flat terrains
A host for the brains
As you kiss the sea with your drains

You sanitize
You clean
You energize
You sustain
Flow you must!

Pain no More

He can't be pained anymore
He's as dead as lead
As a plumber's fingers
Yet with starry eyes a-gaze
Of stern mouth agape
With sides awash with flies
Signalling the patient vultures above
As mongrels lay patiently in wait
Atop dust-mixed gore
With brackish fluid oozing from brutalized flesh

Humanity beholds the fallen figure
In considerable trepidation the perpetrators ogle
As mighty heavens remain silent
In conjunction with Pluto's unknown world
The quiet conspiracy blows stronger
When lesser mortals plucked
From the tree of life
Issues forth the soothing zephyr
To soften the wide acrid expanse
Of living brutality

He is human though
In a world running amuck
As unguided eagerness breezes
So shall the fewer shining lights diminish
Yet the unknown ascending star
In tortuous ascent possesses the sky
As hapless onlookers share in the fleeting joy

Another dawn breaks forth
Amidst twittering birds
Above lowing cows
Surrounded by bleating sheep
Cornered by neighing horses
It's a moment of hope

Under the Tree

In the cover of darkness
I see your likeness
In all its brightness
Without the grimness

Under the tree
With unchained spree
We all agree
To be three

As you draw nearer
I, the emboldened adventurer
Is now cleverer
To overcome the inhibiting conjurer

Your sparkling eyes
My commanded heartbeats
Are now poised to roll in ties
As unguided passion deflates

With leafy branches for cover
So the gigantic stem the guide
As the roots dig deeper
And for once you are the bride

Your touch the warmth
Your gaze the mesmerizer
Our energies burst forth
With murmurings for tranquilizers

We are one, again, under the tree
With a bright moon overhead
We flutter as birds to be free
As we have the earth for a bed

The Mango Tree

It's raining!
They're running!
Wind's blowing!
Leaves are falling!

The stem stands firm
The roots are stronger
The branches are calm
The mangoes are holding longer

The sun is shining
Folks are sweating
The wind is blowing
The mango tree is calling

Folks are standing
Birds and butterflies are waiting
Mangoes are falling
Children are picking

Eager eyes wait
Approaching gazes search
Anxious hearts meet
Disturbed guardians preach

Of busy black ants
Always on the move
In search of plants
In order to stay above

Abdulai Walon-Jalloh

Strained feet on accent
Occupied hands in descent
Pulp juice in streams
Hovering flies clamor in screams

This is the mango tree

The Unreachable Gleam

Caskets of charred remains
Soulless humans
Forlorn citizens

Despicable dungeons
Horrible tales unfolding
Without listeners

Living corpses the cock crows
Alight and disembark
Embrace perdition

Honesty for the dogs
Dishonesty for men
The race unabated

Pendulum smoke
The impossible dream
The unreachable gleam

Reach the unreachable gleam?
Life, the prize
And time-chariot alights

Wurrie

A sprightful lad at five
Under the protection of parents
A wonderful life thrives
In the community eyes

With rushing gaiety
And flushing beauty
To school and mosque
With understanding piety

Wurrie is the name
With achievements to his fame
And a soaring spirit
A fearful bravado frames

A wonderful agility abounds
As heightened intelligence astounds
Amidst the warmth of relatives
And increased communal spirit

At peace with nature
In the embrace of forests
Over the tops of hills
Across cemeteries he transcends

Wurrie the fish of the streams
The birds of the trees
The lion of the hills
The living corpse of the grave yard

Differing Sameness

Let's make
For our sake
In our fate
To relate

The twittering birds
The chirping crickets
The lowing cows
The barking dogs

The shouting children
The quarreling women
The thinking adults
The breezing youths

As in sickness
So it's in joy
As in failures
So it's in successes

From our Maker
We issue forth
And to Him
In our different moulds we return

Apart

It's late
To be mates
As for fate
We're separate

Don't urge
To be plunged
In spite of the surge
To be expunged

Many a time we pretend
Though in few we be
To truly depend
As always we see

Let's be true
For in it there's strength
In our true value
A fabric without threat

As individuals we flourish
In recognition of our distinctiveness
Let's not perish
Yet grow by instinctiveness

The Rainy Season

Over the hills and distant forests
Lightening and thunderclaps attend
The clouds burst open

The drizzle pours forth
With lashing winds
And pelting rains

When grown-ups take shelter
Children are out celebrating
As mothers hurry to the day's activities

It rains and flows
As the swishing leaves
On turgid stems give up

In heavy torrents
Grassy plains are flooded
As soft tubers uprooted

Confused farmers look up to high heavens
With pleading lips and anxious minds
As more rains pour

Folks are out to collect water
As others do the washing
Streams are satiated

The confused and the calm
The starvation and the abundance

Abdulai Walon-Jalloh

The pain and the joy
This is the Rainy Season

Voices

They were here
We were there
As one we walked
As two we separated
Yet voices still linger

Your marks instruct
Our footpaths direct
In the days of freedom
Yet in doses of doom
Our spirits soar

Today our realm in shadows
And as substance in gallows
Reality frightens
Penury strengthens
When it does not smitten

Voices are loud and clear
Yet in ears duller
Shadows loom larger
Essences recede faster
And out of the deep the crawler

Maybe voices are there
As we are here
And together we unite
As in isolation we part
Harken! They say is a virtue!

Wing'd Chariot

Why the hurry
As we ferry
For another cry
With little try?

Why the blame
For the fame
In reckless game
As we tame?

Who is brave
For the save
As we deprave
In our grave?

Who is without
As a left out
To seek about
In the south?

We are inclined
As we declined
The others dined
And we reclined

Nightfall

A hazy overcast sky
As the broods return home
Folks are in reverse gear
Names of children in the airwaves
Cocks and hens hurried to roost

Neneh briskly serves food
As customers bustle for attention
In the dins of plates, spoons and cups
Voices become aggressive and impatient
As the last morsel disappears

The last about deploying
With routine steps
The evening is done
As strained eyes trace out lines on a blurring page
The quiet is dominant as peace returns

Eager voices call out
As numbed joints and reluctant ears disobey
Incessant calls give way to badgering
Yet in a fetal position the night goes by
Love beckons in transitory happiness

It's nightfall
And few are about
As the creatures of the undergrowth chirp away
Of melodious twist and confused haste
Youths idle away into the small hours of another
Oh! Nightfall is gone to come again!

Love

Like nature in the wilds and calm
During all seasons splendid and absolute
Vast in bliss and pain and depth
Evergreen in the midst of turbulence and attrition

In the hearts of mankind you abide
Scarcely you visit in spite of the angst and anxiety

Transience in permanence you betray
Imperious though you stride about
Mysterious you will remain though
Emboldened folks you they readily seek
In the lair of lions
As emptiness permeates their hearts' recesses
Silently you are about
In shine or dark to overwhelm and fascinate

The Light

To the living and loving memory of Victor Fashole-Luke (vfl)

Your light will ever shine
For in our hearts it is always ablaze

Your person we shall always behold
For in our minds you are alive

Yours has been eventful
For achievements galore

Your essence we celebrate
As we crave your peaceful repose

Your departure we mourn
Yet your life will inspire

You are not alone
For you abide in the lord

Reckoning

You need not grumble
When in the struggle
As you are free of trouble
When you bubble

Though they breeze
When in sleaze
Yet in freeze
They will laze

As in hate
They will in joy
For their fate
They will toy

Free

I've got the brains
That's why I'm not in the drains
To be held in chains
And afflicted with pains

Up I float to soar above
In the midst of birds in drove
Amongst the wilds in the groove
And beneath the undergrowth of the clove

In the oceans in the midst of shoals
Afloat on the seas and in the pools
I submerge and crawl
To resurface and prowl

Free in spirit
Loose with secret
Devoid of contempt
Full of wit

Why the Fuss?

They say we're in His Image
As we fret and atrophy
And each other we ravage
And Him we defy

Stay close as death knells
Amidst the frenzy and palsy
And Him we sail to for solace
As our fragmented consciences sally

We ignore the warning
As life's folly betrays
On all fours we come begging
As conscience brays

Are you there?
For it's Him
And He's here
As we swim

Apart but not forever

It is almost two scores
Yet we are still around
Far away from each other
In distant lands
Experiencing dissimilar dreams

Our expectations are no longer similar
As our aspirations are of a different sort
We are of the mundane type
Whereas yours is of the sophisticated kind
Though we inhabit the same planet

Hopefully, our worlds will reunite
In order to bring back fond memories
As we endeavour to celebrate the essence of mankind
Cut out from the same ancestral loins
For to be human is all that matters

Neneh (mother)

The cock crows
Neneh is up

The muezzin declares Fajr
Neneh genuflects in praise of Allah

The BBC Network beckons
Neneh is at her stall

The clock chimes noon
Neneh forages for food

The muezzin announces Zuhr
Neneh prepares lunch after prayer

The muezzin calls for Asr
Neneh is at her stall after praising Allah

The muezzin calls for Maghrib
Neneh is in praise of Allah

The muezzin calls for Ishaa
Neneh prays and returns home

What is my name?

I'm not visible to the naked eye
Yet my presence is always nigh
I'm not an appendage
Yet I cause a cleavage

Mankind usually ignores me
In times of glee
Yet in tribulations
I'm the passage for invocations

You still don't know my name?
Well to many I'm lame
I don't carry the big stick
Yet I prick

The subconscious is my host
Though not a guest
In the quiet of night
I'm about

You must have known me by now!

Abdulai Walon-Jalloh

Feet on wheels

Moving at will
In spite of the ills
Mindful of the prospects
Despite the neglects

The world is yours
As your life thaws
Isn't that wonderful
Though life is rueful?

Since birth you're ubiquitous
Though your every step tortuous
With limited means
Unlimited success attends

You're the child of bliss
Though your every gait confounds
And perils not far away
Yet you soar and sway

You can't stop moving

Childhood

What a time of imperfect perfections
As Neneh and Baba brought happiness to my feet
Amidst trying times
In supposed time of plenty?

In want they toiled
Quietly and patiently they imparted and instilled virtues
With stubbornness and agility, I defied wisdom
And with exaggerated forbearance they manifested tolerance

Those were the days of innocence
As reckless hate permeates our environs
Undeterred Neneh and Baba were indefatigable
Against all odds they prevailed and today I am

Their bosoms my source of tranquility
Their counsels my shining light
Their every mannerisms my very essence
Childhood my parents

It's in your Eyes

It's in your eyes
The daily toils under the skies
And in the middle of the dries
When you hope someone will listen to your cries

You are everywhere
As he will rage and swear
When he tries to bathe and wear
Yet you move your burdensome wares without fear

Some say it's in your gait
As you move through the gate
Your destiny lies in wait
Though you've decided not to be late

Others acknowledge your beauty
For they say your are pretty
As you move across the city
So the chosen few abide in your pity

Many say it's on your back
When they ogle to display their lack
With sham effort they will fill their sack
As you are taken aback

The honest folks see it in your embrace
A touch costly as expensive lace
With the searing burns of an unforgiving mace
As heart's contents laid bare without disgrace

Yet you inspire
Those who aspire
With no pyre
For the martyr

The East-end

A wide expanse of extending frontiers
With rivers and hills on either side
A motley group of players
On the lookout for a ride

What a wonderful assemblage of eager-eyed!
In perpetual state of vigilance
For destiny their hands tied
In continued waste of brilliance

As the nefarious lutenist the companion
Many a hand is pinioned
For want of better opinion
As backs to the walls are positioned

The east-end the home of seminal processes
The backyard of upward progress
During penury the shelter from stress
And for the nude a sort of dress

Punctuated by disappearing streams and cemeteries
With emerging spots for groceries
And decreasing room for pantries
There is an urge for toiletries

Yet the east-end amazes
As youthful energy dazzles
In countless mazes
As the uninspired lazes

Voices and Passions

The seed is sown
When the outer flesh is thrown
The sapling will be blown
As the harvest is known

Yet in abundance the competition
In dearth the promotion
For in frenzy the destruction
Again in bundles the compunction
As the sun always rises in the east

Market Borbor

A noisy ambience
An oyster in its shell
A trail of brilliance
And a fascinating tale to tell

Of scattered stalls
In the shadow of dust
Of wonderful calls
And businesses going bust

As busy bodies are about
In the din of vanishing wares
And a wonderful world of reinvigorating sprout
Of telling and paralyzing snares

In the throng of bodies
Market Borbor excels
Amidst reckless robberies
With reduced moral cells

The sandwiched market
With innumerable exits and entrances
You frame your ingenious rackets
To high acclaim and warm embraces

Your presence is nourishing
To the many that behold
Your physique ravishing

For the multitude in your hold

You are charcoal at night
That burns bright during the day
As you pale off into the star lights
Marshalling the milky moon on its way

Congo Dust

A stretch truncated
As sandwiching gutters speed passed
In the midst of dwellings
As kids go a-crawling

With gold dust a-scatter
As leaves to the ground with a patter
So are eagle-eyed folks in search of laughter
Between murky waters that run with a clatter

As boisterous feet roll over balls
Eager mothers roll out frenzied calls
As anxious stakers engage in brawls

The never-ending noise
The ever active girls and boys
The everlasting resting place for the toys
The home of the abandoned Rolls Royce

Of nocturnal adventurers
Searching for plunders
With no robbers
In confined borders

Voices and drumming
Clapping and stamping
Beatings and crying
Laughter and rejoicing

A new day bursts forth

Folks hurry in different directions
As children hurry to school
Shrill voices issue from goats' horn

Again the balls are rolling
Folks are converging
Masquerades are dancing
Lovers are preparing
As parents are calling

Sierra Leone at 48

I'm in ripe middle age
Facing the difficulties of a new page
Yet I'm expected to be a sage
Though I'm bound in my little cage

I can't take a wife
As little means attend my life
I remain that little knife
That causes occasional strife

I'm still in my parents' house
Though for every passing blouse
My passion is aroused
As my keen eyes browse

Too many children to call my own
Though for many their beings I disown
Yet for all of them I'm known
As I was at the time their seeds were sown

My essence now lies abandoned
As with perverted vigour my being is stoned
Grandchildren keep me constantly loaned
Like the flotsam and jetsam ocean-spawned

Why is my nativity so confusing?
Yet precise convenience is also troubling
Why the hurried labeling?
Is it for universal calling?

I outlast many a pretender
In languid fronting as a bartender
I'm water un-emptied in a cup
A cane-carrying verve at the top

What a bump I carry?
Is water suffused within?
Are my sides streamlined enough?
How bushy and wild my appearance?

Be it then that I'm '48

Freetown Night

A vicious night
As men in wandering flight
In search of ego fight
With little in their fist
As they say; 'it's Freetown night'

It's night-time in Freetown
And the wolves are in town
Discolored with desperate frowns
As the search for the prized crown
As they say; 'it's Freetown night'

These are cold nights
When warm embraces disappear
With hurried steps hurrying out of sight
And the few good men are yet to appear
As they say; 'it's Freetown night'

These are anxious nights
With lone partners remaining open-eyed
As anxiety fades into fright
Their lachrymal faces shall never be dried
As they say; 'it's Freetown night'

They are fulfilling though
As waiting doorway lights glow
And the hurried clatter and patter race along
Entwining welcomes and kisses blown in song
As they say; 'it's Freetown night'.

The wild

I climb to fly
And run to swim under
In the middle of the rain
With so much pain

Birds give way
To my sway
As I swirl
In a while

It's more than you think
With my body covered in pink
And energy in boundless leap
Is tied to my hip

It's the life of a gazelle
Roaming the wild
In a disquieting drizzle
With the innocence of a child

Must I continue with this?
In this time of peace
Thirst within me is on a short lease
As memories gain up in pace

Moments of Glory

Too few are still standing
As the hurly-burly is ending
With diminishing hope
Relying on a long slender rope
Who would dare to venture
The cold ecstasy of adventure?

It's a punishing maze
In a wild blinding flash
That's destined to daze
As paces in restraining marshes eagerly splash
Along in confused movements
Anxious faces in wants
Suspended in temporary animated moments
Like the roosts patiently in wait on top of plants

The book is being read
As listeners hurry away
To a life of dread
In the cold dark way
Waiting for the ominous return
Of a mirage salvation
Engraved in dark old stones
Though, hope, within grows
Strength to discern ebbs
And the moment of victory fades
Like the subdued clatters of spiders' feet on their webs

The distance

A tortuous yet deserving reality
In the midst of turbulence and equanimity
It treats though sublime
In depth and rhyme

A physical separation in body and sight
Yet connected in my mind and soul
Over distant lands and climes
The singing is fresh like grizzly sands in shoes

Painful the void seems
As lingering thoughts emboldened
Against receding tangible presence
Shadowed in locked hearts

In dreams and things
Figures do loom large
To appease and inspire
Against the seething chasm

Objects in the mirror
Closer than they seem
Absence breeds presence
In refreshed memories

The Story of Life

Move nearer to the bashing
With little smashing
In continued lashing
Is a prolonged crashing

Let the oceans roar
And the winds holler
As mankind becomes bolder
So is life's path broader

With calm turbulence
The persistent brilliance
Life's radiance
Without any dalliance

The aspiring driver
Shall possess the car
In spite of the mar
When moving across the tar

Many miles lay ahead
As mouths multiply
Bones and joints begin to crack
Slowed movements continue to bedazzle

The squelching increases
In groaning abundance
With moaning attendance
Life's meaning not a dance

With decreasing chances
Spaces exist in braces
Man understands the paces
In measured traces

Man fears it not
As it's in the lot
For him to knot
Within his plot

Living Reality

It's an oyster ceiling
With cloistered feeling
That was foisting the willing
As toys for a shilling

With wild commendation for their bravery
So was little accommodation in slavery
In spite of the recommendation that was silvery
There was abundant trepidation in each delivery

The sails sallied forth
With pails of sorts
In trails that blot
The veils continue their spurt

On lachrymal faces
With beautiful traces
Leading overflowing tresses
Over deepening creases

The blind lashes and brands
And strands on discolored fleshes
With forced crashes on lands
That cursed with rashes on sands

The wailings persist
As bodies willing to resist
So eager and undying souls exist
Side by side with boundless hope in fist

The living reality
In deserving personality
Is re-living austerity
With perplexing severity

The battle then begun
Is prattle yet begun?
With no title for a gun
So the little attention for the goon

The Road

Sometimes as a straight needle
Running forests in the middle
As encouraged insects fiddle
So other life forms move in trickle

On your heavy surface
Move the bevy face
As machines to some place
Livelihood seekers move in grace

Your mysterious origin
The golden surface
The bronzy outlook
The silvery stretch

Destinations will be reached
As innocence constantly breached
So hopeless souls enriched
Through purposeful sermons preached

As days change into nights
Rains shall give way to dries
As ice gives way to lights
So will laughter usher in cries

Over hills and valleys
Though streams and forests
Under bridges and through tunnels
You shall remain unstoppable

In constant repairing
You receive resurfacing
In gleeful painting
Through ambitious restructuring
Yours is the saddening laughter

Abdulai Walon-Jalloh

Last Line of Defence

As dinosaurs go in smoke
So lizards lie in waiting
For Olympus will grow under their cloaks
Where life is grazing

They flourish too soon
As stars disappear from the moon
And earth's surface in eager anticipation
In frenzied celebration

Where wide expanse of ocean
Sidelined by evergreen vegetation
With rains and sun in succession
It's fecundity in progression

Birds with the sky to themselves
Cadavers and their shelves
Cows and their calves
Salve for salves

Life-forms shall in circulation
Populate in wild embraces
As teeming ants in percolation
Moving in the wild without traces

The enduring identity
The last line of Defence
Till the day of eternity
The centre of reverence

Voices and Passions

This is them
At the helm
Without the phlegm
As they came

In brilliant rainbow skies
Without the lies
The butterfly flies
Without amazing tries

The Truth

In essence
The presence
As conscience
The waitress

It's short
For the strong
As increasing faults
Surely, will prolong

The receding star
On the firmament
Falls from afar
Welcomed by earth

Earthlings in amazement
When nature astounds
In continuous excitement
As puzzle abounds

Configurations in complexity
Simplicity an aberration
As understanding a perplexity
With realism in explosion

A world of simpletons
Overcrowded by turgidity
And clarity the reality
Yet Sisyphus blossoms in turbidity

Dance in the forests

Today when destiny is in its hands
The grasshopper has learnt to be cleverer
When forest fires are out of the lands
And little mention of the conjurer

Weeds and locusts are luxuriating
As innocent plants are choked
When the pain of deluge becomes excruciating
As the swishing scythe is unhooked

The passing winds unacknowledged
As aerating worms unheralded
Tendrils, saplings and tubers dislodged
Bared earth exists to be scolded

The grasshopper remains unyielding
As it increases its mutating genres
Through co-existence and proxy pleading
In false pretences it will pray

With ants for food
Fine-grained dust particles remain deprived
And little favours elude leaves undetached
As sturdy trees remain overwhelmed

So the dance in the forest continues
As the mutating grasshopper lures
The gullible ant pursues
The unreachable gleam contuses

The Race

With speed the haste slows
With broadband the space reduces
With open-ended dishes little remains to be beamed
With so much to spend little left to be bought

With slowness much to be gained
With limited access much to be accessed
With limited antennas anxiety trebles
With little to expend variety is increased

Unlimited success dulls the imagination
As early retirees not in the equation
So is boredom in constant explosion
Amidst diminishing self eruption

Accelerated competition
Overstretched resources
Thinned production
Overworked processes

The brim beckons
Destruction unhinged
Mankind reckons
Elbows bruised

The Real Us

We love to sit
To see others eat
In the heat
And get a hint

When will they stop
To fight at the top
In order to get the drop
And then not destroy the crop?

We at the bottom
Please call us Tom
For we dislike the storm
As it destroys the kingdom

Oh! You phantom gladiators
When will you silence the radiators?
As the air refuses the ventilators
For there will be no predators

We the prey
Shall be free
In a spree
With unlimited glee

An unhindered run
Under the sun
With unlimited fun
For a palm-tree turn

The Era of Men

Which of the sides
Is yet to decide
On those in the inside?

Why the delay
For the replay?
A better display?

It is night
By the light
A fist tight

A big black bull
That is without the pull
In the back of the pool

With circling flies
And baited sighs
The children's cries

The sides are out
To effect the bout
As the bloodied legs sprout

The prize is won
The men folks are sworn
As the costumes are worn

The dust is in the air
As the shouting and clapping clear

The bodies move nearer

That was then
Back in the den
When we were men

The Baboon's Bottom

We love to get by
With the lie
As they try
During the dry

With little to eat
Despite the abundance of wheat
In the middle of the mist
Others will feast

Though we cadge
In a cage
Our little rage
Shall effect rampage

And as trying pleasure
Haunts us in our leisure
So we experience great seizure
In our little measure

Though we be in pain
Yet we do not feign
As we get slain
With hearts free of disdain

Up we float
With light hearts for most
And free cheers for toast
On the right Hand of the Host

Sons of yester years

They say you departed early
Yet it was wise you did
As we begin to question the essence of living
In the midst of gore, tribulation and penury
Sons of yore you were smarter
As our trails shimmer
Amidst disappearing counsel

We are anxious and troubled
In the midst of plenty and calm
As listeners decrease
What a world sons of the present
It's swaying as folks dizzied
At the crossroads of conscience

Bravely your foreclosed your realm
As ours were heralded
In glorious and optimistic note
Yet mystery, confusion and penury abound

Ah! Sons of yore
We salute you in praise
As true sons of the present

Happiness

It's not in clothing and cheap talk
Nor in boastfulness and self-doubt
Though in all I partake
Yet dull to my palate

Peace of mind
For many eludes
Though pleasures unwind
Yet sadness pervades

Again it's not in hideous monstrosity
Amidst an ocean of turbulence
But in tranquility
Guaranteed by eternal providence

It's in the sky
In the middle of the dry
Amidst the chirping
And pleasant twittering

In my eyes
Within my embrace
Your presence entices
My world of grace

Youths

The world is at your feet and fingers
Yet a thousand miles between
Though a touch of moderation bridges
It hardly dawns on you to be

With recklessness you zoom ahead
Oblivious of whom you bump aside
The mirage on the tarred streets recedes
Undeterred by the futility you speed head on

Wise counsel you unheed
And like the stubborn he-goat
You are soup for life at supper
You abhor the reality yet celebrate wisdom

Youth of course you are
And youths of course you will remain
Unless mental maturity sets in
Your efforts to unshackle your beings come to naught

Success

You are on the lips and hearts of all who care
Yet very often your presence is felt
Some toil in vain to succeed
Though your gaze is fixed on others

In vain incantations are made for your person
Yet deaf ears you give to many
How sad and unfortunate importunity remains unheeded
In the early mornings you visit lucky folks

Ah! The not-too-lucky say unwilling farewells at noon
How shall they face dusk with its uncertainties?
Be prepared to face the never-ending realities of dawn
In spite your sweetness many taste bile

But to all success is a mirage
Content to contain it within mind, body and soul
As its sublimity remains a mystery
As undeserving folks bask in its glory

Where have they gone to?

Friends of innocence
In the days of reckless idling
Where are your marks and imprints?
On the sands?

Don't tell me you paled off!

Ah! Now I'm confident
You chose the right path
And brave you are
For daring the unknown
Where the brave of today couldn't tread

Tell me you are high!

Ours is a tale of twisted fortunes
Adulthood in the guise of discoloured faces
Oceans of laments
Listeners far and few in between
Might be good you departed then

We say to you wait for us!

The sun is up on the other side
The bustling frenzy
Of unheeded appeals
Pounding stoned ears
Eyes on heads

Pray for it has come full circle!

Abdulai Walon-Jalloh

The Fading

The sweets
In the streets
Of the east
Are always on the west

Where the nights never end
Wear the best in the year
Wares everywhere for the eyes
We're always hungry
It's never the way it had been
As ever in the hearts of men
Thoughts over the missed days
As the lingering samovar floats into view
Westerly winds blow faster
As diminishing glow hurries nearer
Lazy rivers flow grudgingly clearer
And kids in slow retreat clearer

SIERRA LEONEAN WRITERS SERIES (SLWS)

Focusing on academic, fictional, and scientific writing that will complement other relevant materials used in schools, colleges, universities and other tertiary institutions, the Sierra Leonean Writers Series (SLWS) aims to promote good quality books by Sierra Leoneans writing on any topics and other writers from around the world who write on themes and issues about Sierra Leone.

It is the publisher's hope that students and other readers in Sierra Leone will eventually be at least some of the primary beneficiaries of these works. Not only will people in Sierra Leone be able to read materials that relate to their own lives and experiences, budding writers will also be able to draw inspiration from the efforts of their compatriots and other established writers.

Submitted work undergoes a rigorous peer-review process before being accepted for publication, with an international editorial board providing guidance to writers.

SLWS, based in Warima and Freetown in Sierra Leone, distributes books globally through AMAZON.COM. In Sierra Leone, SLWS books are currently available at the SLWS Bookshop in Warima (near Masiaka) and at CLC Bookshop, 92 Pademba Road in Freetown.

SLWS co-publishes some titles with Karantha Publishers in Sierra Leone.

For further information, please visit our website:
www.sl-writers-series.org
or contact the publisher, Prof. Osman A. Sankoh (Mallam O.)
publisher@sl-writers-series.org

Published SLWS Books
A milestone of the 50th title reached in September 2016!

1	Osman A. Sankoh (Mallam O.)	2001/2016	A Memoir	Hybrid Eyes – An African in Europe
2	Osman A. Sankoh (Mallam O.)	2001	Non-fiction	Beautiful Colours
3	Sheikh Umarr Kamarah	2002/2015	Poems	Singing in Exile and The Child of War
4	Abdul B. Kamara	2003/2015	A Memoir	Unknown Destination
5	Samuel Hinton	2003	Poems	The Road to Kenema
6	Karamoh Kabba	2005/2016	A Novel	Morquee – The Political Drama of Wish over Wisdom
7	Yema Lucilda Hunter	2007	A Novel	Redemption Song
8	Joe A. D. Alie	2007/2015	Research Text	Sierra Leone Since Independence – History of a Postcolonial State
9	Mohamed Combo Kamanda	2007	A Play	The Visa
10	J Sorie Conteh	2007	A Novel	In Search of Sons
11	Michael Fayia Kallon	2010/2015	A Novel	The Ghosts of Ngaingah
12	J Sorie Conteh	2011	A Novel	Family Affairs
13	Winston Forde	2011	A Play	Layila, Kakatua wan bi Lida
14	Eustace	2012	A Novel	A Pillar of the

				Community
	Palmer Doc P.			
15	Siaka Kroma	2012	Non-fiction	Manners Maketh Man – Adventures of a Bo School Boy
16	Mohamed Combo Kamanda (ed)	2012	Short Stories	The Price and other Short Stories from Sierra Leone
17	Sigismond Tucker	2013	A Memoir	From the Land of Diamonds to the Isle of Spice
18	Bailah Leigh	2013	Non-fiction	Dilemma of Freedom – A Diary from Behind Rebels Lines in the Sierra Leone Civil War
19	Nnamdi Carew	2013	A Novella	Tiger Fist – Two Stories
20	Yema Lucilda Hunter	2013	A Novel	Joy Came in the Morning
21	Ebenezer 'Solo' Collier	2013	Research Text	*Primary & Secondary Education in Sierra Leone – Evaluation of more than 50 years of PRACTICES & POLICIES*
22	Gbananom Hallowell	2013	Short Stories	Gbomgbosoro - Two Stories
23	Sheikh Umarr Kamarah & Majorie Jones (eds)	2013	**Poems**	**beg sol noba kuk sup** - An Anthology of Krio Poetry
24	Siaka Kroma	2014	Short Stories	Tales from the Fireside
25	Syl Cheney-	2014	Poems	The Road to Jamaica

	Coker*			
26	Dr Sama Banya	2015	*A Memoir*	*Looking Back – My Life and Times*
27	Andrew K Keili	2015	*Social Commentary*	*Ponder My Thoughts – Vol. 1*
28	Jedidah A. O. Johnson	2015	*A Novel*	*Youthful Yearnings*
29	Oumar Farouk Sesay	2015	*A Novel*	*Landscape of Memories*
30	Oumar Farouk Sesay	2015	*Poems*	*The Edge of a Cry*
31	Gbanabom Hallowell	2015	*A Novel*	*The Road to Kaibara*
32	Mohamed Gibril Sesay*	2015	*A Novel*	*This Side of Nothingness*
33	Yema Lucilda Hunter	2015	*A Novel*	*Nanna*
34	Yusuf Bangura	2015	*Research Text*	*Development, Democracy & Cohesion*
35	Lansana Gberie	2015	*Research Text*	*War, Politics & Justice in West Africa*
36	Yema Lucilda Hunter	2015	*A Biography*	*An African Treasure: In Search of Gladys Casely-Hayford 1904-1950*
37	Moses Kainwo	2015	*Poems*	*Ayo Ayo Ayo and other Love Songs*
38	Abdulai Walon-Jalloh	2015	*Poems*	*Voices and Passions*
39	Gbanabom Hallowell (Ed.)	2016	*Short Stories*	*In the Belly of the Lion – An Anthology of new Sierra Leonean Short Stories*
40	Ahmed	2016	*Poems*	*Along the Odokoko*

	Koroma				River - Poems
41	George Coleridge-Taylor	2016		A Memoir	Transformation in Transition
42	Karamoh Kabba	2016		Research Text	Fire from Timbuktu: A Dialogue with History
43	Umu Kultumie Tejan-Jalloh	2016		A Memoir	Telling It As It Was: The Career of A Sierra Leonean Woman in Public Service
44	Ambrose Massaquoi	2016		Poems	Along the Peal of Drums: Collected Poems (1990-2015)
45	Mohamed Gibril Sesay	2016		Poems	At the Gathering of Roads (Poems)
46	Gbanabom Hallowell	2016		Poems	Manscape in the Sierra: New and Collected Poems 1991-2011
47	Gbanabom Hallowell (Ed.)	2016		Short Stories and Poems	Leoneanthology: Comtemporary Short Stories and Poems from Sierra Leone
48	Gbanabom Hallowell	2016		Poems	Don't Call Me Elvis and Other Poems
49	Bakar Mansaray	2016		Short Stories	A Suitcase Full of Dried Fish and Other Stories
50	Gbanabom Hallowell	2016		Poems	The Art of the Lonely Wanderer

*co-published with Karantha Publishers

www.ingramcontent.com/pod-product-compliance
Lightning Source LLC
Chambersburg PA
CBHW032207040426
42449CB00005B/481